To Jess + Jo

" Happy Trails "

A Lady in the Saddle

by Jean Wilder

Jean A. Wilder

A Lady in the Saddle is part of the exhibit "A Place Called Thorofare: People, Wilderness & Wildlife Management." The story of the lady in the saddle comes from the section "A Trail of Crumbs." The exhibit was shown at the Buffalo Bill Historical Center in affiliation with the Wyoming Game & Fish and the Shoshone National Forest. It was initially shown at BBHC in 2009 and is now part of a traveling exhibit.

ISBN 1466242108
ISBN 978-1466242104

Published by
Jean WIlder
3503 Cooper Lane
Cody, WY 82414

I want to thank my friend Becky Bereman Grimes, who put this book together for me. Her expertise made this book the best it could be. She is a special woman whose talent, laughter and love of life are enjoyed by all who know her. Her flower photos provided the finishing touch to A Lady in the Saddle.

Other books by Becky Bereman Grimes

Leaf Art (lefart)
A Joyful and Playful Look at Leaves...and some poems

Leaf Art ABC...and some dances

Destination: Mammoth Hot Springs for a Very Special Event

Destination: Grand Canyon of the Yellowstone

A Procession of Flowers

From Flowers to Foliage

Bird Tails

Let's Talk Turkey

Giddy-Up!
An original 2010 Leaf Art (lefart) creation by
Becky Bereman Grimes
au@vcn.com

(This book was created while listening to Roy Orbison's Black and White Night concert. BBG)

I cannot say thank you enough to my Mom and Dad who raised me in this beautiful place. The pack trip that they took us on into the Thorofare was a memorable vacation. They nurtured my love of the wilderness and encouraged me to follow my heart.

I have the upmost respect for the Fales family who shared their life with me, teaching me skills that molded my character which will stay with me and the rest of the hands for the rest of our lives.

I would not be the person I am today if not for the experience and the help of each and every one of them.

The Yellowstone Plateau is ringed by high mountains. The big body of water in the middle is Yellowstone Lake. If you look directly to the right you can imagine coming down 50 of the most beautiful miles in the U.S. along the North Fork of the Shoshone River. The smaller, more greenish body of water is the Buffalo Bill Reservoir and Cody is just a few miles past it. The other arm of the reservoir follows the South Fork of the Shoshone until the road ends near the head of the Deer Creek Trail. Due west of there is the Thorofare area in this photo from space. The blue line represents the route through Eagle Creek on the North Fork, through the Thorofare and out by way of Deer Creek on the South Fork.

1979–1996 Rimrock Ranch
Glenn and Alice Fales
Gary Fales Outfitting · Gary and DeDe Fales

WILDERNESS PACK TRIPS

WILDERNESS PACK TRIPS

These horse back trips, with pack mules carrying the freight, take you into some of the finest wilderness back country that is left in the lower forty eight states today. They are totally separate from our dude ranch activities with their own string of horses, mules, equipment and personnel. Pack trippers stay in cabins on the ranch before departing for the back country, if space is available; if the ranch is full we bunk you with a neighbor until the pack string is ready to move out. Some spend several days or a week at the ranch prior to their wilderness outing. Many with aspirations to see the wilderness back country have had their dreams come true by joining one of our pack trip trail rides.

WHEN AND HOW

With reference to time and itinerary, the trips are flexible. However, each trip has to be cleared with the administrators of the Shoshone and Teton National Forest and Yellowstone Park, as regards to the availability of camp sites and horse grazing areas. Even though we can outfit large parties for trips of up to three weeks duration, we prefer smaller groups for lesser periods of time. We like to book one-week trips, with four to six guests. These trips may be routed either of two different ways:

A GOOD SHORT TRIP

The northern trip leaves the forest service corrals and heads up the Northfork of the Shoshone River, with the first camp near Stoney Lake at the head of Bear Creek. A beautiful camp site near timberline, the lake affords good cutthroat trout fishing. From this camp we leave the Shoshone Forest and move into the wilderness back country of northern Yellowstone Park. This country the tourists never get to see, the headwaters of the Lamar River. Anyone can catch a fish in these waters, and see lots of game, as this is the summer range for large elk, deer and wild buffalo herds. A side trip from this camp takes you up Saddle Mountain where you get a spectacular view of this great area. We add as much variety as possible on the return route.

ANOTHER DANDY

The southern trip leaves the corrals at Eagle Creek, making a lunch stop at the falls, and onto the first camp. This creek is full of brook trout, and if you get up early the next morning, you will see moose grazing with the horse herd. Also, this camp offers a chance to explore an old deserted gold mine. From this camp the trail climbs to the pass into Yellowstone Park and lush, tranquil Mountain Creek. The pass offers a chance, if you are lucky, to see the big horn sheep that inhabit the rocky cliffs. In this area we camp on the upper Yellowstone River, which is a great trout stream. A side trip takes us into the Teton Forest and Bridger Lake, and a chance for some great lake fishing. A rubber raft adds some fun to the activities here. This area is as vast and wild as when the Indians came here to hunt and fish, and is miles from the nearest road.

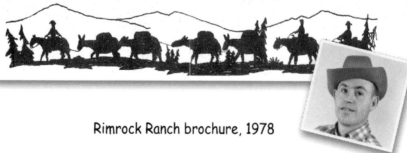

Rimrock Ranch brochure, 1978

2

There is something unexplainable about this country called the Thorofare. It stays with you in many ways, wonderful thoughts and memories of a magnificent country that cannot be forgotten. This land takes you to the Continental Divide where springs bubble up and split into two, eventually heading to the two oceans.

The Yellowtone Delta from Two Ocean Pass
NPS photo

I was eighteen years old when my family went on a pack-trip with local outfitter and dude ranchers, Glenn and Alice Fales. They were a well-known couple who owned and operated Rimrock Ranch. Our trip started on the Northfork at Elks Fork and continued over Rampart Pass into Open Creek. Then we traveled up the Thorofare, over Deer Creek Pass and out to the Southfork trailhead.

Jean Wilder
1974-1996 Rimrock Ranch
Gary Fales Outfitting
Gary and DeDe Fales

My time in the Thorofare was the best time
of my life. Working alongside Alice and Glenn
Fales was an honor. For many years I had seen
his white mule train in Cody's 4th of July
parades. As Glenn would say, "Western outfit,
huh? Not too bad, huh?" Their son and
daughter-in-law, Gary and DeDe Fales, owned
Gates Camp Lucky in the Thorofare and ran
summer pack trips there. This allowed me to
work for both families.

Misty morning over Bridger Lake with Hawk's Rest behind by Jack Richard.

The Gary Fales family: clockwise Gary in the black hat, Gilly, Vicky, Jesse, Jackie and his beautiful wife, DeDe.

Above: Looking up Green Creek to Ptarmigan Mountain.
Below: Looking up Canyon Creek to Rimrock Ranch with Ptarmigan in the background.
Also views of the Main Lodge, a Guest cabin and a trail ride

Not only did they run a tight outfit, successfully running three to four pack strings in the back country, but they also ran a first class dude ranch to boot. The ranch rests upon the north boundary of the Washakie Wilderness and the North Fork of the Shoshone River. Whether you find yourself at Rimrock Ranch or on one of their pack trips you will find yourself being taken care of in the best of style. On day trail rides or a longer trip into the back country you can explore incredible scenic valleys, mountains and streams that the Shoshone National Forest has to offer.

NPS photo

That was the beginning of a lifetime of experiences, meeting all kinds of people, and making memories of top-hands and dude-soured packers. From that time on, I was hired on as cook's helper for $13.00 a day. My duties were cook's helper and camp jack. From the start I loved my job. I loved working with the horses and mules and those stubborn hands, too.

I later became head cook and fulltime summer pack trip cook, eventually guiding elk hunters in the Thorofare. If I was really lucky, I could hunt horns in the springtime, cook all summer with back-to-back pack trips, and then cook or guide during the hunting season. I could work almost six months a year.

Having learned most of my skills from Alice
(who we always called Alice, the Queen of the
Thorofare) and many top hands, I learned how to cook
with cast iron and Dutch ovens. Sims stoves can be
folded up and carried in. Cook stoves were cached in
the permanent hunting camp area.

THOROFARE QUEEN . . . Alice Fales recently celebrated 22 years as a cook in the Thorofare, and to celebrate the anniversary the guides who work for her bought her a belt buckle engraved "Queen of the Thorofare." Mrs. Fales, astride her horse in the back country, spends about two months a year in the mountains cooking for guides and hunters.

The Cody Enterprise, Wed., Nov. 12, 1980

Dunraven Mules &
Unpacking in a hurry!
wyomingtalesandtrails.com

Unpacking
Without
Assistance

Along the way I also learned how to pack panniers
and how to deal with demanding guests or horse
wrecks. I acquired various other skills one might not
find necessary in these modern times, but which up
there could mean survival.

The pack animals are the real part that must not be overlooked. They are the hardest, toughest, and most dependable animals. On every morning that is a move day all the gear, tents, cooking equipment, and everything else from cast irons to dish towels must somehow get loaded into the panniers and packed on the horses by 10AM. They stand patiently as the hub bub around them swirls.

You're alone a lot out there in the mountains...riding, packing and surviving in the back country. It takes a lot of teamwork. You learn to keep things okay between everyone and everything as the days and months roll on. It is different compared to town and cities.

13

Some "camp life" terms come to mind. "Diamonds" are the type of knot we used to pack the horses. As you rode down the trail, you could look back at your string of horses to see if any pack had slipped. So then you could make any adjustments.

Sawbuck loaded with panniers on lead packhorse Deckers with manties on the others.

"Cook's ditty bag" had in it everything but the kitchen sink. Then there was also something we called a "trail shortener" for medicinal purposes.

Don Pond leading a pack string into the Thorofare on a 'catwalk' along Ishawooa Creek to start work on the Thorofare Ranger cabin near Hawk's Rest, August 1952, by Jack Richard.

"Coyoting' was another term we used. Since the Fales had up to four different pack trips going on at one time, sometimes the cooks would cross paths and they would help themselves to my supplies and vica-versa. One time I had to make a trip back into town to pick up silverware since all of mine were stolen. Paybacks were fun though.

Heading into Butte Creek from Deer Creek Pass with the Thorofare Buttes on the right.

The Thorofare was the mid-point to and from everywhere we went. Usually we entered the mountains by way of Eagle Creek and came out Deer Creek. No matter which route we took the wildflowers were always a special treat!

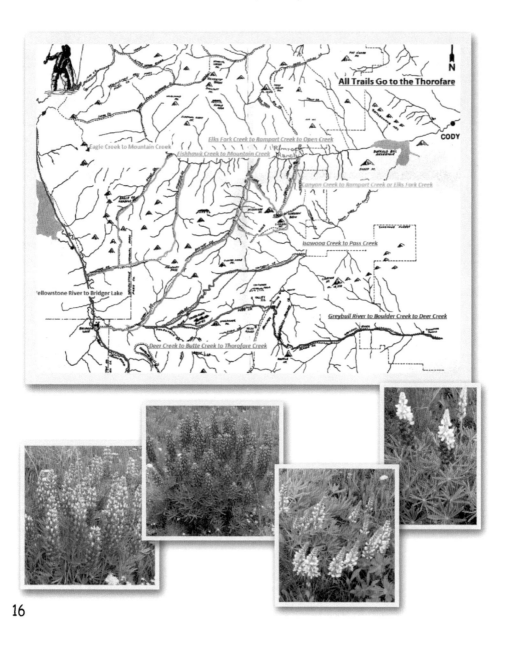

The Thorofare is the heart of the whole mountain area.
How lucky we are to have it in our backyard, basically an
untouched country that is unbelievable and hard to
describe.

Looking up the Yellowstone River toward the Thorofare, 1963
and Bridger Lake, 1959 NPS photos

Bathing in the wilderness is a challenge. Heating water to wash my hair was one thing...

...but baths were taken in ice water run-off in beaver ponds on Thorofare Creek at the height of the sun in the middle of the day, if possible.

Our faithful pack mules stood guard and grazed in the meadows of fresh grass while I bathed.

At times the only real way we stayed in touch with the world was the jets that flew over leaving their cloud white trails in the sky. We were in heaven and the fishing was good in the beaver ponds backed up on Thorofare Creek so we didn't miss it much!

With back-to-back summer pack trips, we tried to take a group in on one side and exchange them for a new group of dudes on the other. After resupplying and, hopefully, an evening in town, we headed back the way we had come out. This cut down on having to trailer the horses to and from the trailheads. Jim Davis, Glen Fale's nephew, gets his white mules ready to go over Rampart Pass in the top three photos on the left. Below there are 4 pack strings moving up and down the steep trail on the Deer Creek switchbacks.

Of all the campsites, the one we called Indian Camp was my favorite. It was almost to Bridger Lake and still in the Thorofare. The camp was on the main trail and it held horses well. Also because of the location of the camp, we avoided the bears and other campers on the lake.

Camping in the Yellowstone, 1886
Yellowstone Camping, 1910
wyomingtalesandtrails.com

If we needed to travel through any part of Yellowstone National Park, the restriction of 25 animals would limit the size and duration of our trips. The 25 would include packhorses, guest horses, and hand horses. You usually had 2 head per person. On the right is Silver Tip Basin.

One summer the snow was late melting so we hauled horses and tack to the Jackson side, which is much lower and easier to pack into because there are no mountain passes. The guests met us in Jackson Hole and Gary Fales rode in from the Thorofare side to meet us and assist with the guest horses and pack strings for the river crossing. The horses were split up so they could swim across the high water one at a time. The extra help was welcomed, and we eventually came out over Eagle Creek Pass, the only open pass on the other side.

A successful trip was one with good mountain passes, healthy livestock, good fishing in the beaver dams on Thorofare Creek and no sores or injuries. A trip like that left you with a respectful feeling of having done your job well.

Horses grazing under Thorofare Butte.

Can you imagine how guests really felt out there with just you as their support system? Can you imagine the giant stories they tell later as they reminisce about their trip to the Thorofare country?

Like this one:

One time Alice Fales was taking a group of hunters out of the Thorofare after a successful hunt. A black bear had been working the top of Deer Creek, and sure enough they came right up on that bear. Alice found a hunter with a black bear permit, and he killed the bear and skinned it right on the trail.

or

The Forest Service asked us to bury a huge old stove that had been left in the area. It must have killed a couple of horses hauling it in and no one wanted to pack it out. We all signed a piece of paper, put it in a bottle and placed it in the oven of the stove. We buried it in a huge hole we had dug.

Prime Rib Dinner
Summer Pack Trip
with Chef Jeanne

We usually had a layover day in which we did not pack everything up and move. I needed a day in which I could prepare this type of a meal which required a good all day fire to bake the prime rib. A 12 or 15 inch Dutch oven would be used. This meant having a cook's fire separate from the main fire which we gathered around. I usually dug a round hole so I could place the Dutch oven down into the ground and use the coals from the other fire to place on the Dutch oven lid.

I always preheated the lids using the main fire. I put the lids directly into the fire until they had completely heated. I never put heat in the bottom of the fire pit. I always heat from the top down. If the coals are placed under the Dutch oven, it will burn whatever you are cooking. Keeping a good fire with the right dry wood makes the difference.

Menu for layover day

Breakfast:
Bacon, French toast and eggs to order,
frozen juice and piping hot coffee.

Lunch in camp:
Hot dogs and buns with baked beans,
fruit and cookies.

Dinner:
Prime rib, potatoes, carrots, and onions and fresh
salad with tomatoes, cucumbers, and dressing.
Blueberry muffins in small Dutch oven.
Orange Jell-O with mandarin oranges, fix as
directed, add mandarin oranges, cover with lid placing
a rock to hold it and place in the creek to
allow it to set up.

Wine and wine glasses.

My favorite time of day was after dishes were finished in the evening, just before dark. You would find me by the river or creek gathering pitch stumps for the night fire. This type of wood burned all night, which in turn kept the bears out. I always had a clean camp with no bear problems when I cooked.

NPS photo

It is difficult to pick out just one trip and memory out of my twenty years in the mountains. Out of all the guests that were taken in on trips, a few stood out more than others. Gary Fales Outfitting provided some of the most unusual memories. One came from the trip we took with Vice President George H. Bush and Secretary of the Treasury James Baker. Along with them came the secret service, a doctor, and a communications man with all of their gear to haul into the back country. Because of security, the hands were not allowed to tell anyone anything about the trip. Having been in the mountains for quite a while, most of the hands were a little homesick.

To Jean Wilder
With best wishes,
Cy Bush

DeDe Fales is between Jim Baker and George H. Bush. Gary Fales is behind Jim Baker in a light hat. Jean is in front next to VP Bush.

At some point during our stay in the meadow, I asked the communications guy if I could make a phone call to my mom. In 1988 there weren't any cell phones but they had a small satellite we had packed in. After that, everyone called his or her mom from the meadow. We also had one fun game of whiffle ball and awarded Vice President George Bush and James Baker, the Secretary of the Treasury, the "golden horse-turd" award.

Scott Mealy, Head Supervisor of Shoshone National Forest gives out the awards.

We were between the Storm Creek and Clover Mist fires in the Lamar Valley when the fires started. Above, packing in from Pelican Creek and below, looking into the Lamar Valley from Pelican Creek Pass.

The wildfires of 1988 brought much discord to the entire region. The early part of the summer of 1988 had started with 2 or 3 pack trips and not a very wet spring. It was quite dry. I was in the Lamar Valley when the fires started and was told to pack out. It was not possible to go down Cub Creek as we had planned so we packed back out to the Pahaska trailhead. At this point Yellowstone's "Let it Burn" policy was in full force. We packed out staying calm and reassuring the guests that we were safe. Our stock was reliable under pressure and we knew they would carry on as usual.

Eagle Creek Meadow with Mt. Humphrey and Mt. Schurz, looking into Thorofare from Eagle Creek Pass.

At any rate we had a trip to the Thorofare. We were going over the pass at Eagle Creek and down Mountain Creek to the Yellowstone River. Here we would go past the Ranger Station by Bridger Lake and then up the Thorofare and Deer Creek. Back then we had no satellite phones or GPS's. It was word of mouth about the fire situation but we knew that the rangers and smoke were sure signs that it might not be the trip we had planned. We would do whatever was needed to keep our guests, our livestock and ourselves safe.

We were packing for a small group of people. I had never been able to stay in the Mountain Creek area because it is in Yellowstone National Park. Bridger Lake and the Thorofare are in the Shoshone National Forest where the horse count could be over 25. By now common sense told us that we would not be able to go through the Thorofare as planned. We would have to change directions and it should be soon...and fast!

There were two possibilities. The first was to go back the way we came, or we could try going to the head of Mountain Creek, top out and find our way over the top crossing the head of Fishhawk Creek and drop into the meadows.

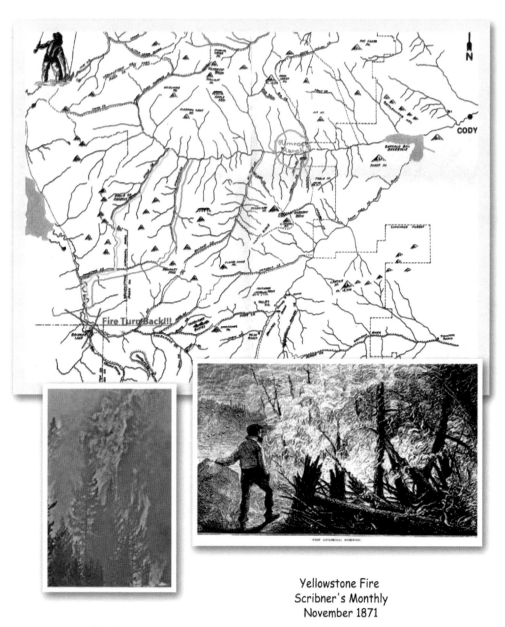

Yellowstone Fire
Scribner's Monthly
November 1871

NPS photo

Head of Fishhawk Creek by Jack Richard

Wow, did this sound western! I sure wanted to be a part of that! Back then Crossed Sabres had a hunting camp up that trail and I knew a couple of people who worked there. I had passed the outfit several times throughout the years especially when they were packing in the gear for the hunting season. So off we go up a trail I had never been on before. I had always ridden by it but never ridden up it into its new and rough country. The Trident Plateau is between the area we were in and the Thorofare.

So we left the white cliffs of the Yellowstone and took a very old, never traveled trail. Maybe a sheep hunter would use it but never any average mountain person. This is a never bothered country, still wild, not touched by man, and may never be touched by man. It is pristine country, the new that is beyond... a beautiful god's country, left alone for the animals. We rode across the top on some game trails.

Mountain Pass by Jack Richard

Then we untied all of the horses in order to walk off the top and work our way down the other side. The trails weren't too bad but were steep with sharp switchbacks. We went slowly, creeping down so as not to kick up any rocks or slip and spook the pack animals. One by one everyone picked their way off.

This is a similar trail to that which we came down. Jack Richard took photos of a pack trip going up. You must know that I had never been in that area before for a couple of reasons. The first was that we always came up from the bottom and never down from the top. Secondly, because of the fire we usually camped in a different area. Here we didn't know where the meadows were, where we could make our camp or hold our horses.

Safely back to the trail we lined back up and continued down. Finally we came to a place where we could gather up the herd. We retied out the pack string carefully making adjustments for each and every guest. It was so rewarding to accomplish and not have a problem.

1920 pack string coming down a rocky trail
by Jack Richard

We gathered up the horses and guests and went on down the trail to the meadow where we would stay the night. The next day we would pull out on the Fishhawk Creek trailhead and trailer the horses, gear and guests back to Rimrock Ranch.

Mt. Shurz by J Schmidt, NPS

When we arrived at the meadow we were quite surprised to find that everybody else in the mountains that summer had literally run out of places to camp and be safe. There were at least 10 different camps in this tiny meadow! We had a lot of horses so it was decided that we would only keep what we needed for one more night so we split up and sent everything out right then. This was a trip we had not planned for and it sure wasn't the usual Thorofare country story this time.

Nevertheless it was our last day on the trail and the last day was always a good day ending the trip. From here we would take the trail to the trailhead ending a never to forget experience. This was my job and it was a way that I could continue doing what I absolutely loved to do and get paid for doing it.

Note from BBG: Dudes were in good hands when Jean was on a trip. While researching for this book I had the pleasure of speaking to people who have spent many hours on the trails and in the mountains near Cody, WY. One was George D. Smith. He had this to say about Jean: "Jean is the greatest mountain cowgirl I've ever met in my lifetime. She is the only other person I know who could tie the Zepplin bend knot."

Later, I was in the back country between trips when a Chinook helicopter dropped me a message to get off the mountain. The last of the horses had been taken out already so the only way out was by helicopter. They wouldn't let me bring my dog along, but after they saw that I was not leaving without him, they relented. As the summer wore on and the fires moved closer to camp our pack trips began to get tighter and tighter. No place was safe. It was a scary and long summer as the fires blazed on. It wasn't long before the Fales and their crew began cooking for the firefighters on the lines.

Between June and August almost 250 different fires started in Yellowstone and the surrounding National Forests. 95% of the total area burned was due to seven separate fires. "Black Saturday," the single worst day of the fires, consumed more than 150,000 acres during one of many firestorms. It was August 20th and it seemed like no end was near. Fires were traveling so fast that they made huge advances of 5 to 10 miles a day, and there were even occasions when they made more than 2 miles in one hour!

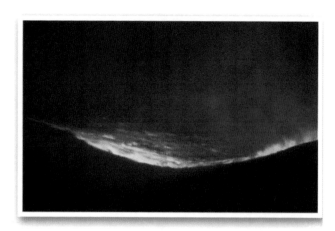

It was the largest wildfire in the recorded history of Yellowstone National Park. Starting as many smaller individual fires, the flames spread quickly out of control, propelled by dry storms which brought howling winds and dry lightning strikes but no rain. The smaller fires grew quickly and combined into one large conflagration, which burned for several months. At the end of July, the National Park Service and other agencies had fully mobilized available personnel, and yet the fires continued to expand. Some of the fire traveled along the ground in the understory until it came to a tree. Then it would climb the tree torching it as it climbed. Other times the crown fires would leap from tree to tree.

Firestorms threatened every corner of the Park so everyone from journalists, cooks and wranglers were required to wear firefighting clothing while in a fire area. If, by chance, the winds changed the direction of the fire you had to be prepared to fight it. These photos by NPS photographer, Jim Peaco, show the smoky conditions in the Absaroka Mountains that form the eastern boundary of YNP. Thousands of acres of wildlife habitat were destroyed. By the next year the forest had begun to regenerate. The first flower to bloom is Fireweed.

The fires threatened several major visitor destinations and, on September 8, 1988, the entire park was closed to all non-emergency personnel for the first time in its history. In the end, more than 1/3 of Yellowstone's 2.2 million acres burned that summer. At the peak of the effort, over 9,000 firefighters and 4,000 military personnel were assigned to the park but were inadequate to the situation. The firefighting effort cost $120 million. These time lapse maps from NASA show the progression of the fires from early July until late September. Yellow and orange designate the Clover Mist fires which quickly merged. The large brick colored fire was the Northfork. In the lower part of the maps you can see several fires that threatened the Thorofare.

NASA/Goddard Space Flight Center Scientific Visualization Studio maps are based on daily ground observations by fire lookouts in the park and by infrared imaging cameras flown over the park at night. These observations are considered accurate to within about 100 meters.

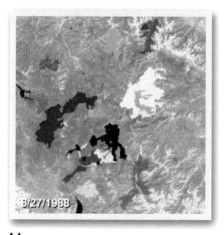

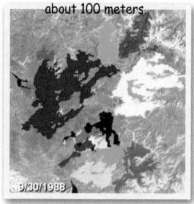

Best and Not so Bad

Best trip...Only one time did my girlfriends from Florida come out and pack in with me. It was so much fun. I think a bull moose fell in love with one of the girls. I shall always cherish that trip with my good friends.

Worst trip...Bugs thick as steel. A special mosquito tent was packed in for the guests, in which they could see in and out. When it is bug season, you better be prepared.

Wettest trip...On that trip I could hardly get my fires hot enough to keep coals for my prime rib dinner. It took forever to cook and we ate in the dark with flashlights and lanterns.

The year 1992 was the first, last, and only time I hunted for myself. I harvested a bighorn sheep. That was thanks to the Fales for spotting it. I had hunted for seventeen days and it finally happened.

One year we came around one of the switchbacks on Rampart Pass to meet a wall of snow. We got out our shovel and dug a trail through for our horses and gear.

One time we were doing Jackson trips and someone left their knife from lunch sticking in a tree. He told me where they had lunch and which tree it was in. Three days later I rode in with my dudes and we stopped for lunch in the same meadow. I walked over to the tree and took the knife out to return it days later.

Buster Brown

I bought a wild horse from the Fales. His name is Buster Brown and he is at least thirty years old. I have had him his whole life. He is now in retirement and keeps company with two five-year-old bay colts from the McCullough Peaks area and a new yearling named Star. Star is a sorrel mare with a flax mane and tail, and she loves it here. I have handled and broke my last three wild horses. I have a passion for them, and I believe they are great horses for this kind of country. They never tire or quit on you when you are crossing mountain passes and ridges. They are dependable horses, and they are there for you when you really need them.

Buster poses here with Cheyenne and Red during my sheep hunt on the backside of Gobbler's Knob.

Going over Butte Creek Pass and looking into the Thorofare.

Every time you top over Deer Creek Pass and look down on the Thorofare, it is like magic. The valley opens up and you can see for miles. It is a certain kind of accomplishment to be able to appreciate this country in my back yard. So many locals have never been in the backcountry. The feeling of being truly at home surrounds me as I pass through this God-given country. I always say, "Hello, Thorofare" or "Goodbye, Thorofare," holding back the tears of gratitude, pausing only for a moment to say a prayer.

The Thorofare is an area that you must pack travel to get to. You can pack through Eagle Creek, up and over and then down into the Thorofare. Nesting in the Park the year of the fires was very different than normal. You learn to make do just as you must do in life, crossing bridges as they arise. But my point is-to get to the Thorofare was just a huge task, and I loved it. To move through our back country and experience that life and be filled with awe of such beauty is amazing. It takes a certain type of person to do that type of work and those of us who did it formed relationships that were, at the time, built on survival.

This view looking west up Crow Creek to Yellowstone Lake shows Cody Peak left of center. The large mountain to the upper left silhouetted against the lake is Avalanche Peak, and the island in the lake over the head of Crow Creek is Stevenson Island. The craggy peak along the upper right edge of the photo is Silvertip Peak.

Fales' career honored

By MAGGIE SHEPARD

A Cody man has joined the ranks of Sacajawea and Jim Bridger in the Professional Guides Institute Hall of Fame.

Life-time Wyoming resident Glenn Fales was inducted into the Outfitters Hall of Fame on June 10 at a Lake District annual meeting.

In an awards ceremony at Lake Ranger Station in Yellowstone, Dick Clark of the institute presented the award which read, "Glenn kept the spirit of the West alive."

Clark named Fales the "patriarch of Yellowstone outfitting in his own day." The institute's three-member Hall of Fame is based in Dillon, Mont.

At the same dinner, Glenn and his wife Alice were honored with the Howard Eaton Award — another first as this award has never been given.

According to Lake District Ranger John Lounsbury, the award remembers Eaton who was one of the earliest Yellowstone outfitters, serving the area around the turn of the century.

Not until 100 years later did park officials find someone who earned the award named after this "big, looming figure for out-

Rimrock Ranch outfitters Glenn and Alice Fales recently won the first Howard Eaton Award for their life-long dedication to outfitting in Yellowstone. Glenn was also inducted into the Outfitters Hall of Fame. (Courtesy photo)

fitters," as Lounsbury described Eaton.

"Glenn and Alice were the first ones, so we're setting the bar pretty high," Lounsbury says. "I wanted it to be given to somebody who has done a great deal of good work operating in Yellowstone. We really felt good honoring this giant of an outfitter who has been guiding in the park since 1967."

Fales, now 80, was born in

Deaver and grew up in Garland, his son Gary says.

After running a business in Meeteetsee, Fales acquired Rimrock Ranch near Wapiti in 1955. He outfitted from Rimrock for 42 years, but Gary says his father guided for nearly his whole life.

Touring Yellowstone Park and the Shoshone and Bridger-Teton national forests by horse, Glenn had many guiding partners throughout the years.

"Almost every noted guide out of Cody has worked for him," Gary says.

And he also worked for his share of noted guides, Gary says, including Fred Garlow and Ned Frost.

After hearing about the awards, Gary says his father was pleased and felt honored. He was unable to attend the ceremony, but Alice went and gave a short acceptance speech.

Cody Enterprise, July 14, 1999

I just can't say enough about the whole outfit. Glenn and Alice were the best people to work for in this business with Gary and DeDe following suit. There is a strong work ethic that is evident in the way they do things. I have had nothing but respect and appreciation for all of them and the people I worked with. It is a tough and trying job, always on the move. We continue to learn about and love the country we witnessed and lived in.

49

The greatest and best time of my life was working in the mountains. Over the years I worked for many outfitters in this country, but the Fales ran a western outfit. Riding for the Lazy Rockin' A and riding into the Thorofare was the most beautiful time of my life. Each year it was like coming home again!

I loved it when either boss, Glenn or Alice, went on a trip with us because of the camaraderie and spirit they both had. It was always a pleasure. We (the hands) called Glenn "Chief." He was a wonderful man and we miss him. "Hey, hey, hey!"

Heading for home!

As I look back on my many years of working in the mountains, I now realize what great opportunities I had living life in the wilderness. I yearn to return, just like the many other old-timers and packers in the area do. Many of those have moved on and many are still in the Cody country.

I would like to thank the Buffalo Bill Historical Center, the Wyoming Game and Fish Department, Shoshone National Forest, Yellowstone National Park, Dude Ranch Association, Park County Historical Society, K.T. Roes, Charles Grimes and Nancy Stranger and especially, the entire Fales family.

Thank you all!

Basic Summer Pack Trip

Cutting board
Silverware
Plates
Cups
Glasses
Soup bowls
Skillets
Wilson grill
Wash pan stand
Stove stand
Meat
Steak
Fried chicken
Prime rib
Smoked pork chops
Ham
Hamburger
Tuna
Roast beef sliced
Salami
Lettuce
Tomatoes
Shrimp chow mein
Pickle relish
Margarine
Candy bars
Coffee
Kool-Aid
Frozen juice
Dishpans (2)
Water buckets (2)
Coffee pot
Dippers (2)
Stove propane
Pitchers
Tablecloth
Table
Toilet paper

Napkins
Kitchen pans (nested)
Kitchen utensils
Matches
Shaving cream
Dish soap
Sandwich bags
Bologna
Shrimp canned
Sausage
Bacon
Bread
Dinner rolls
Hot roll mix
Bisquick
Blueberry muffins
Carrot muffins
Raisin nut muffins
Corn bread
Date nut bars
Bread
Crackers
Hot chocolate
Cottage cheese
Chocolate pudding
Salad dressing (Italian & Ranch)
Fruit Jell-O
Macaroni & cheese
Cole slaw dressing
Cheese
Enchilada casserole
Sour cream
Hors d'oeuvres
Triscuits
Wheat Thins
Fritos
Freezer tape
Flashlights
Honey
Tea
Salt & pepper
Serving bowls
Potholders
Ajax
SOS

Chore Girl
Hand soap
Clothespins
Can opener
Dish towels & rags
Hand towels
Lunch sacks
Toothpicks
Garbage bags
Clocks
Dips & sausage
Cookies
Frozen cake
Cheesecake
Chocolate mint pie
Pancake mix
French toast batter
Vegetables
Mushrooms (Lg & sm)
Spanish rice
Corn
Asparagus
Green beans
Peas
Potatoes
Pork & beans
Carrots
Celery
Radishes
Onions
Green peppers
Cucumbers
Zucchini
Cabbage
Mandarin oranges
Cantaloupe
Pears
Peaches
Apples
Applesauce
Oranges
Bananas
Tropical fruit salad

Basic Kitchen Camp Equipment (for 25)

First aid equipment
Oxygen tank & mask
Penicillin
Penicillin needles
Nose drops
Bufferin
Syringes
Bourbon (2 bottles)
Plates
Soup bowls
Cups & silverware
Serving bowls (3)
Sandwich bags
Lunch sacks (100)
Freezer tape
Stove
Propane
Mantels (7 pkgs.)
Lights
Flashlights
Clock
Matches (1 carton)
Radio
Lime
Saw
Whip rake
Horseshoes

Syrup bottle
Tablecloths
Pepper shaker (1)
Garbage sack (2)
SOS large
Clothespins
Ajax
Pot scratchers
Washbasin
Dish pans (4)
Hand soap
Washcloths
Hand towels
Dish soap
Dish towels
Dish rags
Pot holder
Game tags
Elk license
Meat sacks
Pencils
Aluminum foil
Toothpicks
Toilet paper
Paper towels
Thread & needles
Shampoo

Hair pins
Scissors
Cream rinse
Deodorant
Toothpaste
Magazines
Stationery
Overshoes
Can opener
Meat grinder
Presto cooker
Pans
Cake pans
Pie tins
Sq. head griddle
Pancake turner
Fry pans
Coffee pots (2)
Water bucket
Dipper
Butcher knife
Mixing spoon
Egg beater

Spike Camp
Big Horn Sheep Hunting

Coffee pot
Dish soap
Sq. head griddle
Plates
Cups
Silverware
Dish pans
Dish rags
Pot holders
Coffee
Matches
Fire starter
Lantern
Grill
Grate
Frying pan
Pancake turner
Can opener
Toilet paper
Towels

Packed horse with panniers
by Jack Richard

Hunting Camp Food

Cream cheese
Cheese
Cottage Cheese (3)
Oleo (10#.)
Whipped topping
Coffee (3-3# cans)
Tea
Hot chocolate (Swiss Miss)
Eggs (30 dozen)
Milk (2 lg. Boxes)
Crisco (1-3#can)
Oil
Salt (2 sacks 5#)
Cookies (9 pkgs.)
Flour (5 sacks for bread)
Baking powder,(1 can)
Brown sugar
Honey
Pancakes mix (2-10#)
Hot roll mix
Stove Top dressing
Blueberry muffins
Gingerbread (3)
Cornbread (4)
Piecrust (2)
Cherry pie mix (3)
Apple pie mix
Blueberry pie mix (3)
Chocolate cake (2)
Yellow cake
Cake frosting
Fudge frosting (2)
Jello puddings
Pepper (1 lg. Can)
Nutmeg (1)
Cinnamon (1)
Sugar (2-5# bags)

Carrots
Potatoes (2-25# sacks)
Hot peppers
Toothpicks
Catsup (1 gallon)
Pickles
Jelly (1 gallon)
Olives
Vinegar
Salad dressing
Syrup (2 gallons)
Popcorn
Peanut butter
Candy bars (6 boxes)
Turkey (1 cut in half)
Pork chops
Meat loaf
Stew
Barbecue ribs
Dry beans
Sweet potatoes (fresh)
Steak
Roast
Chicken
Ham
Roast
Turkey roll
Tuna casserole
Chili
Chicken broth (2 cans)
Chicken noodles
Lasagna
Barbecue elk ribs
Chicken & noodles

Macaroni
Spanish rice
Small meats
Lunch meat
Tuna
Ham
Chickens (6)
Pork chops
Roast (10#)
Bacon (2 slabs)
Sausage link (15 lbs.)
Steak (17)
Stew meat (8 lbs.)
Spaghetti & sauce (2 cans)
Crackers (2 # boxes)
Soups
Tomato soup (6 cans)
Bread (12 loaves)
Pork & beans (1 case)
Fruit (fresh & canned)
Pineapple
Jello (3 lime/3 fruit)
Raisins
Juice
Large fruit (3)
Peaches
Cranberries
Vegetables
Dry beans
Celery
Lettuce (10 heads)
Fresh tomatoes
Sweet potatoes
Instant potatoes
Cabbage
Onions
Stroganoff
Spaghetti
Taco casserole

Made in the USA
Charleston, SC
26 June 2013